2024
TEJASWI KOLLI

One Love

Copyright © 2024 Tejaswi Kolli

All rights reserved. No part of this publication may be reproduced, distributed, or transmitted in any form or by any means, including photocopying, recording, or other electronic or mechanical methods, without the prior written permission of the publisher, except in the case of brief quotations embodied in critical reviews and certain other noncommercial uses
permitted by copyright law.

Table of Contents

Mini Cooper - 2 Door 1

Meet Cute 5

Beautiful British Columbia 11

Chapter 1 – Follow Your Bliss 15

Chapter 2 – Presence, Practice, and Participation 29

Chapter 3 – The Path to Eternity 45

Chapter 4 – The Way to Your Heart 59

Chapter 5 – Come as You Are 67

Chapter 6 – Lets See How The Cosmos Work 75

Chapter 7 – Who am I? 83

Note from the Author 91

You Don't Really Have to Read This 95

Mini Cooper – 2 Door

I first met her in North Carolina, where she got me a nameplate: EBT-5**2, First In Flight. Then we moved to New Jersey, the Garden State, all her cousins live there, and I got a new nameplate: H**-PWT. Now, I'm in Vancouver, but she hasn't given me a new nameplate. I was so excited to get my new nameplate, "Beautiful British Columbia," and drive her around the city.

I warned her in my own way. I reminded her about the number plate whenever she took a walk. She said she had no intention of getting me a new plate and, if they gave her a fine, she would simply pay it or apologize and explain the situation.

She is just upset, how will she explain that to an officer?

Anyway, she had different plans for me. She parked me in the marked lines of an underground garage, left me all alone, covered in dust, and stalled in the dark. She even forgot the parking stall number. For an entire year and a half, she didn't know where I was, how I was doing, or if I was alive or dead.

She never treated me like this before. I know her better than anyone else. She was polite and treated me with respect, always smiling when she looked at me. If I was distant, she would visit me. Distance never mattered to her. She always knew where to go, especially for the people, things, and places she cared about.

What pissed me off was not that she wasn't allowing me to drive her around the city, but the fact that she acted as if I didn't exist for an entire year and a half, as if she didn't know or own me. I was just somebody to her.

I mean this is a girl who walks miles to hug a tree in the forest. That's my girl, she will do anything to get another glance of what she cares about.

She walked miles in the forest, did roundabouts with her new bike along the seawall, took Ubers around the city, and used e-scooters for shopping. She started taking pictures of fancy new cars. She does have good taste; I mean, she picked me without a test drive.

My entire existence is all about her, and she knows that. I stayed quiet because I understood her more than she understood herself.

She is upset. "You brought me far and further. I don't like coming to Vancouver; I didn't want to stay here for more than a month or two. After waiting for three months, I did this to you. I distanced myself from the memories of you. You are punishing me for no reason."

I know that. I know the number of jobs she did three month-long tests and trials only to turn away at the last minute with knots in her stomach, just to avoid coming here north, but I brought her anyway.

I told her, "Listen, even if this is a punishment, it's a beautiful one: North Shore mountains, orange juice in summer, hot chocolate in winter, blue ocean, quiet coffee corners, fancy cars, sky-high apartments, and the company of wise old trees in the forest. Who would complain about that? Look at the birds and squirrels, how they come close to you. You always wanted that for yourself."

ONE LOVE

That's what these little humans do, they pray for miracles to happen and when they happen they act like it's no big deal. If only I could count how many miracles have been overlooked by these little who-oo-mans.

She said, "You brought me here for your own reasons. There are a lot of you all around me. All these ice-blue Mini Coopers—you just brought me here to meet your friends."

I said, "That's not true. I didn't even know there were so many of me until I came here. I don't like that there are many of me. I wanted to be the only one for you. On every road we drove, we never saw any others. I always felt rare and special, just for you, to make you feel special and rare."

She shrugged and said, "It's a good thing, right? You are not the only one. There are many of you everywhere, and they are all special in their own ways. You are not alone."

Between you and me, I'm not the humble one, and she knows that. I told her the same.

"Of course."

"Listen, I want you to be safe, and I felt you would be safe here," I quietly said.

She looked at me, didn't say a word and left.

We are opposites When I say 'No', she says 'Okay'.

∞

Meet Cute

When we first met, I was standing next to a red car. The car dealer was giving her hype about the red car—this, that, blah, blah, blah. I bet she didn't listen to one word. She was just looking at me, excited to meet me, with a very friendly smile. I knew I didn't even have to say a word to please her. She looked at the car dealer and said, "I'll take this one." He was upset and worried for her; he didn't want her to choose me. He even felt sorry for her. He reminded her, "You have to pay a high cost; it's not really worth it, but it's your choice."

But what is there to trade in between us anyway, she is already there with me without much asking. I know that she doesn't really have to pay a big cost for me. She can afford me with a single penny. But the girl isn't really grown up enough to know all that.

She gently said, "But it's my car; it's mine."

I was hers before she even owned me. That's her—she knows me without knowing me.

I was curious to know. Mostly about her intentions.

I asked, "How do you know me?"

She replied, "I saw someone like you at my university, and then I saw you in a movie. One day, while working, I had this little déjà vu moment. I saw you in a dream, almost like a daydream, but it felt very real. It's like I met you before even meeting you. Little moments added up, and I recognized that it's you."

"It's called manifestation, a little human secret—to love something from a distance and, one day you have it."

"Hmmm. Humans and their little secrets."

"They must already know more than a secret. Actually, they aren't here to seek secrets at all; they are here to seek the truth."

"I thought humans were well aware of that."

There were many opinions about her first car. Friends and family gave their own judgments. Her brother laughed and said she just went and bought a new toy from a toy store. Her parents knew she was going to buy me anyway; somehow, they knew she would find someone like me. After all, she shares every single detail about her life with them.

They know her better than she knows herself, just like I do. Nothing that comes out of her mouth is really a surprise for them. They can guess whom she is hanging out with, what she is eating, what she was feeling, her likes and dislikes, mundane chores, everyday habits, and what time she went to work—everything.

But she is changing; she is growing up. Her dad complains now and then that she is hiding things from him. So, he stopped talking to her and started questioning her more, in countless ways. So, he gets his information.

ONE LOVE

Her mother always finds a way to know her. Even now, she may take some time to share, but she shares everything.

She used to share everything with everyone, including me. Slowly, she started to hide, not because she wanted to hide something, but because she didn't understand many things, situations, and people. She started observing more. It's a good change, a positive one.

I'm telling you, I brought many changes into her life—so much sunshine, so many rainbows, fireworks, good friends, good opportunities, and good habits too. I took her to a silent retreat for ten days in Atlanta.

Our first trip together was to Asheville, her favorite place on the planet right now—one of many. Every time she visits Mount Soma, she says to me I have someone here, who makes me feel I am not alone.

Anyway on our first drive to Asheville, her dad made her stop the car every hour at a gas station; he didn't sleep the entire night. He just wanted to make sure she knew how to drive safely. Four hours isn't much, but for her, it is.

Her best friend taught her to drive on the highway and told her she was ready for her first solo trip. After successfully completing the day trip, if there is one thing I realized between her and me, it's that I am the one who needs to be safe. She has no intention of keeping me safe; she is a little rough.

But I changed her to be a smoother driver. I made her compete with trucks, and we won every single time. I allowed her to eat breakfast while driving to work. I made her drive fast, cross traffic signals just in time, and stop right before the danger trap. She drives fine, but amateur in her own way. I can handle what she can't.

When her mom came to take care of her in New Jersey, she said, "She is a very smooth driver," and I took the credit. Every time someone recognized her by the car, she would come and tell me; she knew how to pass on the credit and compliment.

I slowly took control of her life. I didn't allow her to walk much. I looked one step further than she could. I took her to places, made her meet people, and then brought her back safely home.

I made her feel safe. I didn't allow her to hang out with the wrong crowd. I didn't take her to many parties. I found a way to stay away when she went out with the wrong crowd on weekends. I always went to pick her up as early as possible.

I stopped them in my own way—some people don't fit into her life or my vessel. Every time she carelessly gave me to someone to drive, I did something to make her realize that. I once stopped the engine until she apologized. She knows she can't keep me dirty for long, she can't give me to everyone, and she can't go to every place she wants to. I make sure she knows it; I taught her discernment.

I know the people and places she will have fun with. I know her best friend too; she drove me as well. They both share the same birthday. I know all their early morning to-do list calls while driving to work and evening conversations before they go back home. They went to cinemas, ate popcorn, read books, visited ice cream shops, sang songs, laughed a lot, and traveled together. They used to stop in the middle of the road and wonder where to go. They are very bad with maps.

Between you and me, they don't talk anymore. I asked her the reason. She said, "We have grown up and grown apart. There isn't much to share; we don't have anything in common. We are on different journeys." It makes sense to me—it's normal, but people miss people, and they can live with that.

I heard that once they read a book until the middle of the night and decided to go to the beach to see the sunrise. They are so bad at spotting the sunrise that they drove until 10:00 AM to see it. They are that bad. I know that story. I also know she missed the sunrise at the beach camping with her roommates too.

I want to make sure she finally sees it and checks it off her bucket list here in Vancouver. When she does, she'll understand why she's missed it so many times.

I have her itinerary, and she knows that too. I'm not just a vessel with wheels; she sees more than that in me. She may not know me too well, but she has never treated me like just a vessel with wheels, and I've never treated her like a mere bag of flesh and bones. We truly take care of each other.

So, I took some of her decisions—where she will go, how much time she will spend there, and where to go next.

To be honest, I'm always one step ahead of her. I see what she cannot see, clear her path, and make a way for her. I make her understand that I am one step ahead to clear her path forward to home.

She is upset because I made all her decisions.

I didn't allow her to find home in the wrong places. If necessary, I took her to places a little late and brought her back home a little faster than she wanted. I had my ways to get to her. I can freeze her, bring tension to her feet, make her feel restless, tell her that we got to go somewhere, that mum-ma is waiting, it is time to eat, there is some work still pending, you need a good bath, its time to go to bed for a night of good sleep. If only she knew how I always made her go on and on until she runs back home from everywhere she goes.

I took more than a minute or two, dropped her willpower to zero and made her drive a little slower if she tried to take a detour to go back to someone she knew.

I have my own ways of making her miss what she is supposed to miss. I made her give up waiting for someone and talked her out of never ending conversations. I know who likes her and who dislikes her. She doesn't know, but I do. I saw their faces in my mirrors and maintained a distance because I had to. I made some big promises to her parents: I will always bring her home safely with a smile. With me by her side she is never alone, even if she pretends to be.

Her dad demands that she do the right thing always, and her mom wants her to be kind at all times. But she doesn't always have the capacity to do so, all the time; Sometimes she needs a little more help.

She says it's a little more painful than she thought. I agreed but reminded her kindness and righteousness will help her grow. These are growing pains, and your pain will always have a purpose, I promise.

The girl has to learn everything by herself—how to buy groceries, how to cook—while being criticized for not knowing it already. She actually thought her first job was paying her pocket money. So, I have to step up and make some big decisions for her.

That's not all.

I also moved mountains to ensure she met the people she needed to meet, even if only for a moment. So, If she had to meet someone, I made sure it happened. I knew how much time she needed to spend with them, and once the time was up, I took her away. If someone means something to her, they mean everything to me, because she loves so dearly.

See, I'm not someone who can claim that I did all the right things for her. But I know that I did more good than harm. I did both good and bad for her best interest and everyone involved. I took her through the wrong doors if she had to, but never allowed her to stay there.

Good grief, I can live with her complaints, but I can't live with her regrets.

Beautiful British Columbia

After a year and a half, just before returning to our new home, she came to me quietly. I didn't respond; I acted like there was no life left in me. She was a little worried, called a mobile mechanic, and asked him to fix me. He didn't have to do much, but he acted like he did. She believes in these people, but I don't.

Then she called someone to come and clean me. He took me out of the garage and drove me into the sunlight after many months in the dark. He gave me a thorough bath, took all the time in the world, and removed all the dust, gave a good shower, and filled me with new scents. I asked her to give him an extra tip, so she did.

She quietly said, "It took me a lot of time to find you in the garage." I didn't respond. She embraced me like a child and started reciting the Hanuman Chalisa. "Why are you singing that?" I asked. "I learned it for protection," she said. "I'm singing it here so that you stay safe too."

I took time to be her friend again. Not that I don't trust her, but I wanted to let her know that I missed her in my own way. She missed me too. Finding our way back to each other came naturally to us; we didn't have to force it. We were there already without even trying.

That's what gives me the hype. She gets me like nobody else does. Even in our first meeting, the red car was trying to get the dealer to sing praises about its glory, and she was already there with me. I didn't have to make any trade with her. We share an inheritance of love, and she knows it. I know it too, but I don't show it often because I'm afraid that if I do, she might not see beyond me, and she won't let me see it either.

We both share that fear. We both knew we had to go beyond ourselves and find more than what we already have. We didn't come into each other's lives to bind us together but to set us free. That was our challenge: to find more of what we already have within us, to go above and beyond, and see how much more we can discover.

We knew it was a very big challenge to go beyond each other, but we signed up for it because if we didn't, we would lose our way, our path to eternity.

∞

She found a cruise with "Princess" written all over it. It made her smile and reminded her of me. Then she looked at the G Wagon; it almost looked like my big brother. She even had a picture of an ice-blue Bentley; it was almost like my reflection.

"It's like I'm running away from anything that reminds me of you and coming closer to everything that makes me feel closer to you," she said.

I looked at her and smiled. "None of them. You haven't found what you're supposed to yet," I said.

"But I liked them all," she replied.

"Because they remind you of me?" I asked.

ONE LOVE

"In a way, yes."

"See, that's exactly where you've got it all wrong," I said.

"How?" she asked.

"If you keep looking for me in them and have them because they're kind of similar to me or make you feel closer to me, one day you'll realize they aren't me, and that's how you end up getting hurt," I explained.

"Makes sense, but how do I go beyond you and find something else? Going beyond you means losing you again?" she asked.

"No, to go beyond me means you have me; you're looking for more of what you have found in me."

"What did I find in you?" she asked.

"sat-chit-anandha..*"*

"The eternal state of bliss,"

"Sat-Chit-Ananda" means:
- *Sat: being*
- *Chit: in awareness*
- *Ananda: of bliss*

"Then tell me more about it, as humanly as possible, more like my story than yours.

Dear, your words, my words, your language, my language, whichever way you say."

∞

CHAPTER 1

Follow Your Bliss

SAT- CHIT- ANANDHA

Remember the meal your mom cooked for you just before you started preparing for your exam? That's the nature of bliss—grace that takes care of you, inspiring you to go on with the journey. No matter how far, how difficult, or how long, you can begin from here because someone gave you something to make you feel good enough, and you are ready for the journey.

Oftentimes, this little bliss accompanies us when we can't really see what's ahead of us, when we feel a little alone, until we make it to the other side of what makes us feel vulnerable. For now, imagine this bliss to be a glow of amber, a little star, a ring of a rainbow, or just a little spark.

Epics, mythologies, marvels, fairytales, and prophets are all about its grace— inspiring us to go through everything that makes us feel very insignificant, yet still making us feel strangely powerful while going through it, because we are on the journey and we will figure it out. When we make it to the other side, they will recognize us by our bliss.

"You have that spark, don't lose it." Words in the mouth come very easily.

But we know that little spark doesn't make our life easy or comfortable. It makes us see the truth we aren't ready to see, takes us to valleys we never knew, gets us into dark tunnels, and even threatens to disappear if we don't agree with life.

Good heavens, just to save this little spark, to keep up with it, we keep changing our ways, our attitudes, and sometimes our entire lives. If we allow it to take center stage and give it permission to lead us, it goes above and beyond to transform us, plotting new trajectories, igniting us into new purposes, and changing how we align with ourselves, work, people, the world, and the cosmos.

When I say cosmos, it feels like a very big word in my mouth, but then, we are all part of it, and this little spark makes us feel so. That's exactly why we keep up with it, to feel like we belong. No matter where we go, we remain beloved, brightened, and blissfully beyond.

The most beautiful part of this story is that the little spark meets us right where we are. So, if you are on the adventure with your little spark and you made it this far, then this is the way forth: force, flow, fly, and be fine.

Create space

Now, where do we pull this magical little spark out of nowhere or everywhere we go? How do we grab it, keep it to ourselves, and make it work for us?

It's very simple.

Look at the blue sky.

ONE LOVE

Wherever you are, try to find a place where you can just be with yourself. I wake up every morning, take my bike, and cycle to a prospect point. But on my way to this prospect point, I found a place where I can just relax and be with myself. I can hear the birds' songs, see the ocean, and just lay on the grass. In a place like this, I can just be. It's easy to be in my bliss.

This is how you know you've found your space:

- You don't want to leave that spot.
- You feel at peace.
- You feel a connection to everything around you.
- You don't feel like looking at your past.
- You don't feel like knowing anything about your future.
- You don't want to fix anything.
- You feel seen, heard, and understood as you are.
- You feel okay.

While you are in this space, you will naturally stop checking your phone and stop checking the time. This space reminds you when to leave. I promise, it will never allow you to overstay. If it asks you to overstay, there is always a reason for it.

Remember when you create spaces like this, where you can just be, you will naturally walk into the rest of your day carrying that grace, come what may.

The ones who built the bridges across the ocean, fought battles they didn't choose, carried mountains to sustain their clan, and traveled roads not taken, they are made of this grace. You can see it in their face.

Replace your complaints with questions

The easiest way to stay in bliss is by being in gratitude. If you are in a place where you aren't in a position to be in gratitude, the next easiest thing to do is to question. By questioning, you try and look. If I am not seeing what I am trying to see here:

- Where can I find it?
- When will I find it?
- How do I identify it?
- Why am I here?
- What is it that brought me here?
- Who is it?

So many questions, so many answers, so many ways, and so many opportunities. But by complaining, we close our own doors. Because the simple law of complaining is: I am refusing to see the grace, I am refusing to see life the way it appears to me.

This is life, and so many things happen for so many reasons. But questioning helps. It's the medicine. The easiest way to make the best out of everything is to take a pen and paper and ask.

Before you try and fix something that doesn't look okay, do not go to battle with anything that makes you feel unsettled. Sit with yourself and write your questions. Ask everything and everyone on your paper: When, Where, What, Why, and How?

Question to introspect.
Question to find answers.
Question to understand.
Question to realize.

The easiest way to navigate yourself back to your bliss is by asking questions.

Spend time in nature

If you aren't your favourite company, then the next best company you must seek is nature. Some days in life, we need someone who is more than a friend, a person who sees through our darkness and still be kind to us. Nature has a way with us; it sustains our ruins and recovers us back to life.

We run through cycles in life as long as we live, and we walk into challenges without an alarm. There are so many things, perspectives, and mysteries that have been kept from us about our own lives. It takes years, and sometimes decades, to form a perspective, to get a complete picture with a human mind.

Nature is wise; it has an order, it understands seasons, it knows cycles, it has been here from the beginning, and it has been through everything that a human can possibly go through in a lifetime, once, twice, thrice, everlastingly so. We must understand that nature knows us more than we know ourselves. Maybe it's just part of creation like us, but still, it knows us more than we know ourselves. Spending time in nature makes us little wanderers; it's very easy to unlearn here. In the presence of wisdom, unlearning is inevitable.

So, before running into the world with pain and confusion in your heart, go back to nature. Lay down in the mud, soak your feet in the river; it knows how to tame your wild, bring order to your mind, and change your path towards the divine. If I had to write a list to give you a perspective on how nature helps us, I would be a fool. So, I will keep it simple.

1. Nature is very kind.

2. Nature teaches us connection.
3. It sees us through, with everything we are, and everything we will ever be.
4. Nature helps you strengthen your connection with your cosmic beam, your little spark.

So, when you are alone or a little lonely

It's inevitable to encounter loneliness between experiences. Sometimes, even when we have everything, there is a sting of loneliness.

There are some journeys we have to take alone. There are some people waiting for us. There are some people leaving us because they have new journeys to take. Alignment happens according to the journey we are taking to complete a life that is promising.

During crises, we often feel extremely alone, almost as if we are battling our own spirit to feel seen, heard, and understood.

We refuse to acknowledge ourselves or our purpose because we believe life isn't reflecting what we feel about ourselves—we're not where we want to be, or life isn't reflecting the real us. Sometimes we give the best to a person or project and still feel they didn't see it. However, a personal crisis pushing us into loneliness is a perfect opportunity to strengthen our connection and trust with our inner spirit.

It's not the absence of inner spirit or light but our refusal to see its value that makes us feel alone. We elevate everything in the external world while dismissing our own spirit as insignificant. It's time for balance.

Reestablish your trust with your spirit.

Instead of giving up on everything that makes you feel alone, focus on what doesn't make you feel lonely. Instead of blaming a situation, place, or person for your loneliness, navigate through activities and connections that alleviate loneliness. Talk to people who care about you. Don't focus on closed doors; see who opens a door for you. Remember, this too shall pass.

Do not give up on yourself.

During tough times, when I didn't know how to navigate loneliness, I simply stayed awake all night to watch the sunrise. It was important for me to see the sunrise after spending a night alone with myself—it symbolized hope. Some days I would watch the sunrise, grab something to eat, and then go to sleep. No matter what, I would stay awake until I saw the sunrise. That was my fight, my personal win.

Go and sit in a place where people pray.

Sometimes our biggest problem is not with others but with a higher power. We cannot accept loss or defeat, and we blame God, destiny, or the universe. I did too. A friend of mine shared that her dad, during a deep financial crisis, would go to the temple every day and sit there until he found the hope to stand again and get to work. So, go where people pray. You don't have to ask or believe in God; just being in a positive, communal spirit can rebuild us.

Be safe and protect yourself.

Loneliness can bring up emotions, triggers, fears, and overthinking. It's a purge process; release what gives you pain and makes you feel defeated. You might not create your best relationships or solutions from loneliness, so resolve the loneliness first. Don't indulge in anything that makes you feel weak. Even in bad times, lean into your little spark wherever you see it.

Be gentle with yourself.

When no one else is making an effort to see, listen to, or understand you, do it for yourself. Your life is valuable to you and your loved ones.

In loneliness, you are creating a new connection with yourself, finding new ways to talk to and see yourself. You are trying to be with yourself because you see your light, you know it has value, and you have something to offer the world.

It is very important to have a strong connection with your spirit and nurture it like a mother nurtures a child. The nature of this connection must be one of unconditional love.

A kind word: I came from a culture that celebrates farmers as first citizens. So, in their language, don't discard your bare land because you had a bad crop. For a farmer the crop is of value, a treasure, but the soil is sacred.

Be all about love

So, talking about unconditional love in a world of cause and effect isn't really cool. But it's available to us. If we ask it to show up in a way we want to see it, by our conditions, we are just missing the magic of it.

As an adult, you might doubt its existence, and sometimes it's difficult to know how to love, but the child in you knows love; it seeks it everywhere. Now, if you can turn around and give your inner child some love, will it cause any harm to you?

The easiest way to help the little child in you is to find joy in every waking moment.

So, if you can paint a wall, cook a meal, pray, grow a plant, or go for a walk just to feel the satisfaction of it, your inner child will wake up to joy.

Like on a holiday, just to see the sunrise, eat breakfast, and listen to birds sing, how easy is it to find joy? How easy is it to appreciate?

To clean a really dirty room and make it beautiful, you have to start somewhere. One patch at a time, by giving yourself completely to deep cleaning, you will soon feel you have the cleanest room possible. The adult in you might find happiness in a clean room, but the child in you gets joy in rubbing off the dirt and playing with the water.

So it is with painting a canvas, cooking a good meal, going for a long walk, or dancing in nature. Every time you make something just for the feeling of that simple joy, your inner child feels very, very happy because you are playing with the vegetables, going outside of the house, and playing with colours.

If you are in pursuit of something truly unconditional, you don't have to look too far; it's right here. Appreciate the flowers on the sidewalk, the sunset, and the sunrise. The more you appreciate everything around you, the more you will start to appreciate yourself. You will not be afraid to look back. You will not be afraid to look forward.

Day-dreaming

Daydreaming is a luxury. Talking in a mirror and saying sweet nothings to make yourself smile is possibly the best habit. There is a world available to you only in your dreams, and it is magical. Only in dreams we try to look at our best selves; we dream of everything we could ever be. When we dream, we smile. To have a smile on your face is a real deal you make with life.

To daydream and make vision boards, to take a pen and write to-do lists, give yourself another goal, plan a week, month, and a year, make picture journals, write wish lists, find songs that speak to the dreamer in you, make your playlists, watch movies that inspire you to new realities, find people who can dream and inspire you and collect quotes that will speak to you. In how many ways can we dream? We can even dream with poetry, write letters, and just by daydreaming, we can deeply love what we actually love.

Dreaming, manifestation, the law of attraction—whatever it is, it is a true art. It helps us express without holding ourselves back. It helps us to claim ourselves back into new realities. It helps us like a map, like something to hold on to, to claim ourselves from deep waters and stand on our feet again and again. To get a grip on ourselves and get going wherever we are meant to go.

Dreaming helps us find a connection with a life we actually love and care about. It gives us an opportunity to handcraft our life with love. If there is a dreamer in you, there is a visionary in you.

Give a chance to the little boy or girl in you to dream again. Let it handcraft its own character, values, mentors, things, people, places, and most importantly, keep your faith in what you actually care about.

True treasurer

Look at yourself, you are the treasure and the treasurer. Let's recap and see why I called you that:

You know how to find your spark out of nowhere.

You know how to nourish your connection with your spark.

You are friends with it, a very good friend.

You know how to give yourself to nature and receive its help.

You protected yourself from loneliness and isolation.

You know how to take care of the child in you.

You know how to dream.

You can actually question.

You can actually appreciate.

You have your smile back.

You know how to love yourself unconditionally.

You know where to go when you want to be seen, heard, and understood.

You actually have your own inner world, your true territory where you can generously be yourself without any kind of validation, and that's just like any superhuman living in two worlds.

Positive. We can put together a life of our own, hand-made with our own efforts, gear up to get to our finish line by going the extra mile if we must, making dreams come true, bringing happily-ever-afters to our destiny, making a good story to share while looking at our favourite pictures, making possibilities out of every impossibility, and rising from every catastrophe. How?

∞

"So, once I have the bliss, I will have you forever? That's it?" she asked.

"That's not all. It's more than that," I replied.

"Its not just about finding me but its more about where you are leading me into?"

"What does that mean?" she wondered.

Like when you took a flight, found the bike, then the e-scooter, and learned to walk, and then swim. You went to places where I could never take you in my four wheels. You were stretching my horizons, allowing me to be more than what you saw of me, you were giving me freedom to be, instead of trapping me into the pictures of fancy new vessels that came your way.

While you were doing that, I was resting, dreaming of you in my own ways, talking to my friends and sharing all your adventures, and we all laughed. While you were relaxing at the sea, I am sleeping here.

ONE LOVE

Taking the deep rest I needed after taking you to North Carolina, Florida, Rhode Island, Boston, and New Jersey. I didn't have rest; I've been running on my wheels all my life.

"But you could have done it all alone. Why do you need me?" she asked.

"We need each other until we don't need each other, that's the deal we made."

It made her sad.

So, I told her, "To let you know that what you see, I see too. What you sing, I can hear too. Wherever you go, I've been there too, in my own way. What you do to yourself, you do to me too. If you're careless with yourself, you're careless with me too. If you're reckless with yourself, you're reckless with me. Where you are leaning for comfort there you are leading me too. So, if you seek the company of good people, I will have it too. If you have good habits, I will have them too. If you do good work, I will do it too. If you are taking care of yourself, you're taking care of me. If you look in the mirror and smile, you're smiling at me too. If you love yourself, you're loving me too. If you're protecting yourself, you're protecting me too. What's important to you is important to me too."

More than anything else, I'm here to remind you that wherever you go, I'll be there too, endlessly. To remind you that out of everyone, you are never alone. You are rare, precious, a reason for my smile, something of value to me. Because with you I am there in **sat-chith-anandha**."

"So, all those ice-blue Mini Coopers—they are all you?" she asked.

"Yes, and the cruise, and the Bentley, and the little ice-blue Beetle, the little squirrel that came your way to make you smile bright, whatever that brought you into **sat-chith-anandha**. I show up like a rock, a pebble, like a blade of grass, and a tree you are sitting under, in my own ways. Because you allow me to."

I can see you are trapped in this vessel of wheels for me, how do I set you free?" she wondered.

"Just like you were trapped in this bag of flesh and bones, when you can be free," I replied.

"So, if I set myself free, I will set you free too?" she asked.

"Aha…" I said, with a knowing smile.

"How do I do that?, How will I set us free?"

"Oh, the same old answer I can give, by being there in **sat-chith-anandha**."

∞

CHAPTER 2
Presence, Practice, and Participation

Now that you have that little fire, that little spark, the inspiration, and enthusiasm to embrace it, you will be more than ready to go out there and offer it to everything and anything that is of value to you.

My dear friend, this is the time you need to know how to protect that little spark. How to invest in it, how to ignite it, and how to nurture it.

There is a difference between blissfully aware and blissfully ignorant.

Remember the story of The Jungle Book, when King Louie asks Mowgli to give him the little fire, the little spark, because with that spark he can do wonders and make his dreams come true.

"Together we have powers, all the jungle's treasures ours. You got the fire and I got the desire," were his exact words.

Now, you need to have self-awareness or help from someone to identify people who come to you for your little spark. To trap you into their own ways and limit you into something they knew.

The little spark is here to lead you to see the best, forgive the worst, forget the bad, and maintain faith.

So that you can inspire and ignite that spark in many, nurture them into their true happiness, true potential, and inspire them to take the right course of action.

So, take a step back

Now that you know there is something that takes care of you very well, you might be ready to face the world as you are. While that is the goal, I encourage you to take one step back, two steps back if you can, ten steps back if you must, and twenty steps back if it's possible for you.

As humans, we long, we desire, and we like to take our lives into our own hands and make things happen for us. It helps us stay in control; problem-solving fixes us, and giving explanations makes us feel validated. We need to be in every room, every meeting, and experience everything we possibly can. We have to fulfill so many promises, and we are ready for it.

Once we know that we are being taken care of, once we know we are following our bliss, and the little spark is alive within us, we want to use this spark to get what we truly want. We want to invest it in something that holds value to us—family, friendship, work, and purpose.

It's inevitable to have that feeling because now we know we are truly taken care of.

Here, you need to take a step back. We have to look within ourselves to understand why we love what we love.

Remember that song you picked up from a friend and kept singing the entire day?

Just like that...

Suppose there's a song in our hearts. We give it our voice and sing it aloud so that our own echo finds its way back to us, however it's meant to find us. We call it our song.

That's us, all our lives, just trying to listen to our own echo in the name of accomplishment, wish fulfillment, and dreams come true.

But what if that song we're connected to isn't actually our song in the first place?

What if everything we love in these things, people, and places are echoes of a song that we just kept repeating because we picked it up somewhere and we just don't know how to drop it?

I know we all need that song to make the most out of ourselves. So, I am not asking you to drop the song; I am just asking what you will do with an echo without knowing who is calling?

We call it self-introspection.

Before you pick up your next goal or make a new friend, try and look within to see as much as you can.

Here and Now

Be a legit "here and now" person. Look at the people around you. If memories take you down a path, go back and see what you need from that story, but then come back here. If your dreams take you into the future, go there for a minute, take that ride, but then come back to this moment.

So much happens in the present moment. If you can connect with it, stay with it, and be fully present, you will overcome overthinking, anxiety, and the fear of missing out.

Take a day off. Decide from the beginning of the day to the end of the day that you will stay in the moment, live in the present, and connect. If you have a partner or friend who will join you in this little ride of staying in the moment, partner up with them. Start with the sunrise and end with the sunset.

There is a very slight difference between observing and consuming. If you stay in the moment, you lean into observation. If you deny the connection with the moment, you lean into consumption. So, strive to connect with the moment. Between your stretches, your walks, and your cooking, try to see if you are in connection with the moment. If you connect with the moment, you will align with the cycle of the day and become more curious.

Remember the rabbit hole Alice found out of nowhere; it's not just a story.

Connecting with the present moment will help you see beyond the surface. There is so much of life hidden from those who cannot connect with the present moment. The stones are alive, the grass is alive, the ocean is alive, the mountain is alive, the rain is alive, and the sky, the sun, the moon, and the stars are all alive. Being a genuine "here and now" person is your ticket to experiencing life that you missed while surviving the past, the future, people who lost you, and people who haven't found you yet.

If you like it, do it every day. If you are a busy person, find moments to connect. If you are so busy that you sometimes forget to breathe or eat, then take a day off once in a while just to be a "here and now" person.

Journal

Journaling helps. If writing your thoughts doesn't come easily to you, drawing stars, flowers, or simply rambling on the paper also helps.

When you see a blank page, what do you want to do with it? That's the question.

What does it make you feel like?

- You can write your goals in BIG letters—what you can prioritize and what you cannot.
- You can write your problems in BIG letters—what you can solve and what you cannot.
- You can write the names of the people that come to your mind in BIG letters. What did they give you and what did they take away from you?
- You can even write random words like Joy, Gratitude, Pain, or whatever you feel like.
- You can write your favourite quotes.
- You can look around for a while, stay distracted.
- You can just cry about something.
- You can draw lines and ramble upon them like a child.
- You can write about something that you actually don't relate to.

The most fun part of journaling is that you can create your own template. You have permission to be yourself on a blank page. I sometimes use my journal as my own magazine. I might even write a recipe. Be comfortable with a blank white space; allow it to reveal yourself slowly. It gradually removes your guard and allows you to be yourself. Then you will see for yourself what needs your presence and what needs your absence.

I usually sit in coffee shops while journaling. It gives me time for distraction and time to be with myself. Believe with all your will and might that you are here for a reason, and once that reason is fulfilled, you will enter another season.

Set your Intentions

No matter who you are, what you're about, or what goals you want to achieve, setting intentions is your zeroth step, your core.

In India, we call it Sankalpa—an intention before we begin. Even before we pray, we set an intention.

Here are a few examples:

- From here, only good and auspicious things will happen.
- To protect and nurture goodwill.
- To live, love, and laugh.
- For the highest good of everyone involved.
- Divine will, divine intervention, divine protection, divine grace, and divine support.
- Forgiveness, recovery, and redemption.

An intention isn't the first step; it aligns to zero and has the potential to set your path to infinity.

The way intentions work is to amplify, diminish, expand, and contract.

If you set a goal, you will look forward to a result. But if you set an intention, it will help you find the path, pick up the goal, and then decide the nature of your success.

If you quietly state your intentions and let them unfold, they will quietly do their work and allow you to do yours.

This means an intention has the power to move mountains for you or to make a mountain out of a mud hill.

AUM

Ever wondered what the sound of life force is? It is AUM. Keep your mouth wide open and say AAAAA, then bring your mouth to form a small circle and say UUUU, and finally, close your mouth and make a sound HMMM…

The sound AAA connects with your GUT.

The sound UUU connects with your HEART.

The sound HMMM connects with your THIRD EYE.

This simple sound helps you connect with your life force. This little life that you have—you want to protect it, keep it together, have control of it, and nurture it to harmony, abundance, and goodwill.

Ever wonder what keeps this entire universe intact? Sages and gurus from India believe this is the sound that tunes life force into the universe we live in. By attuning to this sound, we will be able to be in the right place at the right time.

Practice it 11, 12, or 21 times.

One of my classmates in school used to write OM, a shorthand for AUM, all across her notebook to bring her focus back to her studies and to pull herself from any distraction.

AUM slowly and steadily helps you reach your infinite potential, and your potential is divine potential. People who chant AUM become brighter and are emotionally very balanced. If you are a believer, AUM helps you navigate God's will for you. AUM helps to make this body, mind, and spirit your comfortable home.

As long as you are chanting AUM, you will feel safe, secure, and will navigate your way by God's will, evolving to His infinite potential.

Every human, every species, including aliens, and everything in this universe—mountains, oceans, trees, stars, minerals, and more—responds to the sound of AUM.

I just want to say this to you: the entire universe resonates with a sound, and it is AUM.

It's the only secret you need to know. Go and whisper it in your loved ones' ears as often as you can: AUM.

Self care

We all need some nourishment. Our mind needs it, our body needs it, our thoughts need it, our story needs it, and our breath needs it too.

The zeroth step here is to form a connection with everything that you want to care for mind, body, spirit.

ONE LOVE

The first step to any kind of nourishment is always to remove toxicity and toxins.

The second step is to bring beauty into your environment.

The third step is to maintain a balanced approach between what needs to go and what needs to stay.

Now let's see how we can apply this to our body, mind, thoughts, and story.

For your breath:

- Breathe out and then breathe in.
- Spend time outdoors and indoors.
- Find a breathing exercise that you can easily adapt into your routine.

For your body:

- Keep it clean.
- Renew your energy through activity.
- Practice fasting.
- Eat healthy and fresh food.
- Maintain good posture.
- Stay hydrated.
- Rest, relax, and sleep well.

For your mind:

- Meditate.
- Sit still.

- Use your breath to help you focus.
- Take breaks between tasks.
- Catch yourself from overthinking and lean into the present moment.
- Listen to simple music.

For the story in your head:

- Look in the mirror and practice self-talk.
- You can choose to empower yourself or disempower yourself with the stories you tell.
- Use journals, vision boards, and pictures to tell a new story.
- Listen to new music.
- Use affirmations.

Here is an example of an affirmation:

"I allow divine protection and support. If I cannot control it, God's grace will. I am precious to someone, brought up to be of value, a reason for a smile or two, kind, nurturing, a home, sanctuary, and goodwill."

Whether it's your breath, mind, body, or story, use it to empower yourself and direct yourself toward your own goodwill. Take your power back and use it for your own good.

Encourage yourself to take the first step, to reach the finish line, to achieve prosperity, success, happiness, love, and be all smiles.

Chanting

Ever since I was a child, like many Indians, I was encouraged to chant. Chant as if your life depends upon it. I chant my way into every room, every workplace, before I rest, before I take an exam, and before I receive my results. Chanting is an escape for me. It helps me divert my focus from what is controlling me. Chanting relaxes me and helps me fall asleep. If I drop a wallet, I will go back searching for it while chanting. It's simple: what you are searching for, trying to achieve, or going after can be approached with ambition, worry, excitement, or simply through chanting because you don't know what to expect, what is good, what is right. So many times its safe to loose than to consume. By chanting, you call upon the divine to handle the challenge before you, and sometimes that challenge is the restless monster within yourself, seeking something to feed upon.

By chanting, you tame the beast within you, whether it is within your reach or beyond your perception. This beast could be fear, agony, blame, aggression, restlessness, subconscious fears, or any attack, and sometimes even pure ambition—anything that drives you wild and out of your senses.

Before you chant, understand that the intent is to allow divine to lead the way. It means you are okay with listening to a No. Greed has no place in hearts of people who chant, it humbles you.

Meditation

Sit with yourself comfortably in silence. Please don't make mediation another goal to achieve. Di you ever long to sit with yourself, listen, and be be kind to you.

Meditation requires three things:

1. A comfortable posture to sit in.

2. A quiet environment.
3. An intention to listen to your silence.

Make it a regular practice. Close your eyes and see how long you can sit with yourself. If you fall asleep, it means you need that sleep. But continue with your meditation practice. Meditate to spend time with yourself. Meditation helps you reclaim pieces of yourself that you may have lost in the past, in future aspirations, in the people you love, and in your work. It makes you feel whole. Once you are comfortable with yourself, it helps you find the whole world within you.

The goal of this chapter is to be in solitude. To be with yourself, and not lose yourself in everything that you touch, see, speak, and listen to. I promise you there is a beautiful world out there. A destiny only you can fulfill. A love that is very kind, people who truly love and admire you, countless wonders, opportunities, and many people to guide you to your destination. I promise you there is a way to a better world, better people, better situations, and better achievements.

But make peace within yourself, we got a long road to travel, we can do it one day at a time, at our pace. We know what's driving us crazy is devil anyway.

Solitude

The gift of self-introspection is solitude. It is the ability to spend time with yourself, to feel your emotions, and then to tame and nurture them into something auspicious.

Solitude means having a deep and beautiful connection with yourself. You can talk yourself out of a bad story and into a good one. You can accept, contemplate, and reflect on every single detail of your life.

You have a genuine connection with the moment you are living. You can smile effortlessly, redirect your thoughts effortlessly, and help yourself effortlessly.

Here are the signs that you are in solitude:

- You give attention to the present reality, environment, and people right in front of you.
- You take a moment with yourself before absorbing or indulging in any positive or negative thought, word, or action.
- You focus on what needs to be done rather than what's stopping you from doing it.
- You have the ability to transform every curse into a blessing, one step at a time, with grit, goodwill, and divine grace.

Achieving solitude is no small feat. A person with solitude shines like a diamond with crystal-clear intentions, clarity, and charm.

I promise you, no matter what you achieve, whom you marry, or who you become, whether you sit in the forest or in a room full of people, you will shine like a diamond. You will know what to take, what to leave, what to give, where to take from, and how much to give. People will want to be like you—not because of your profession, partner, or work, but because of your simplicity, serenity, and clarity.

You just have to ensure that you keep your inner world intact. Protect it. I have given you much information on how to build and protect your inner world and how to bring yourself back to solitude without needing to act in the outer world.

Once you have solitude, indulge in it. If someone needs your comfort, give it—don't hold back, but don't overshare. Do what is needed and let it go.

If you are in solitude you will realize, People need very little of us. Sometimes a smile, a happy picture, and most of them times just a hello.

Now you are ready for the next step, next goal, next relationship, for your family. You are prepared, and you don't have to look too far.

Your ground is nourished, moist, alive, and very healthy; now it's time to plant your seeds.

$$\infty$$

The girl looked at me, her eyes full of wonder, and asked, "Yeah, how do I do that?"

I responded gently, "By walking the path."

She tilted her head in confusion. "A path?"

"Our path," I clarified. "You didn't just appear randomly, like a fallen angel at my doorstep. You met me because you are on the path, and I am on the path too."

"It's like a map," I continued, "infinite in telescope, ∞," We are dedicated to it. It's like a song of our home. We keep singing it to come together as many times as we can. So we can come back home to each other, a bit closer than before, be one with each other, and then go far and further."

"Well, Why do we come together and go away from each other?

"To bring you closer to your own heart. So, that you will know who you are, what you care about, and stop pretending who you are not."

"That's the path. Who are you and What do you truly care about?"

She pondered for a moment and then asked, "So, how do I stay on the path?"

"You need to lead by example and keep looking in the right direction. If you seek the company of good people, I will have it too. If you develop good habits, I will have them too. If you do good work, I will do it too. If you make good decisions, I will make them too."

The girl looked thoughtful. "And what happens if I do all that?"

I smiled and said, "You go through everything and become something everlastingly new. You rest and relax, knowing that there will always be a way for you to an endless eternity because you care for yourself, care for me, care for everything you are engaging with, and for an endless universe."

∞

CHAPTER 3
The Path to Eternity

Manasaikam vachasaikam karmanyaikam mahatmanam

Translation: "The great souls are those whose mind, speech, and actions are one and the same." Once upon a time, there was a prince named Ram. His beloved wife, Princess Sita, was taken away to a faraway place called Lanka by a wicked king named Ravana. To rescue her, Prince Ram needed to cross a vast ocean.

Prince Ram and his army of monkeys prayed to the ocean for help. The ocean provided them with a map. They collected stones and pebbles and wrote "Jai Sree Ram" (Victory to lord Ram) on each one. Working together, using all the help in reach, they built a bridge across the ocean. Through this journey, Prince Ram became the hero he needed to be.

Prince Ram and his friends crossed the bridge, defeated King Ravana, and rescued Princess Sita. They were very happy to be together again.

Magic words

"I can" and "I will" are the only magic words. The ones who went to the dark side of the moon, the ones who built a bridge across the ocean, and the ones who carried mountains on their fingertips.

On this planet, under this blue sky, if there is any magic that has ever happened, it happened with these two words: "I can" and "I will."

So, use these words, and put them into action. You have to do the work; you cannot escape it. Do it once, do it twice, do it thrice—do it as many times as you can, as if you were born to do it. Take rests in between, relax if you must, pick yourself up if you must, tell yourself the magic words, "I can" and "I will," and do the work. It will be done, one step at a time. You will build a castle for yourself, a bridge between two worlds, and you will become the work you have put in.

The mountain you made out of a mud hill, the mountain you carried on your back, the mountain you moved, will make you a mountain. I promise you, if you do it one step at a time, you will get there. Say the magic words again: "I can" and "I will."

See what calls for your attention and what calls for your distraction.

When you are doing yoga but feel the urge to dance, you get into dancing, that's how life works.

What we think we have to do, what we need to do, is sometimes, or maybe most of the time, is in conflict. If we have a plan in hand and it leads us to a dead end, know that it's a detour.

While you are thinking of solving a problem, but feel the urge to cook and eat, please, by all means, go ahead, cook, and eat. When you get back to your work, you may solve it better than you did before.

So, here, dancing isn't a distraction. A detour isn't taking you out of your path, and cooking isn't taking your focus away. It's just redirecting you to a better place, a better state of mind, a better space. That mistake you made while trying is only teaching you a lesson.

That little kid, trying to get all your attention, while you are working, is not your distraction, he will lead you to a beautiful world that you probably cannot perceive, all by yourself because you are thinking.

Then what is distraction?

A distraction is something that makes you feel that you aren't enough. That friend who laughs at you because you didn't dance at a party, who snubbed you because you didn't want to drink alcohol, who doesn't listen to you even after you gave a long explanation for doing things the way you do naturally, is a distraction.

Did someone ask you again, why do you smile, always?

Everybody knows who you are—everybody. Some see it, some help you be it, and some, with all their true capacity, try to dim or steal your light. You must be aware of all these distractions, please.

The main goal of distraction is to make you feel you aren't good enough, that it can't be done, and that it's not possible.

If you have fun at this party, you are a fun person. If you wear that dress, you will look great; that's their language. If you get that job, you are successful. No matter what you do, there is always something else you must have done—that's the language of distraction.

The tools of distraction are simple: self-doubt, criticism, gossiping, bullying, asking for explanations, baiting with your validation. But they all have the same nature: to make you feel there is something fundamentally wrong with you, that by doing a certain action it will fix you. This is the core nature of distraction.

So, my dear friend, there are people in this world who will make you laugh, dance with you without music, friends who protect your dignity, take comfort in your smile, and there are clothes that fit you comfortably. There are people who will sing songs with you when they run out of words. More than anything, there are people who want to see you shine, who listens, help you introspect, and help you navigate your way forward.

They don't say you are not good enough. Instead, they make you feel better about yourself and remind you that your dreams and goals matter. The best people in life are always free. The ones who make you feel there is a cost to pay will always be costly.

Find your rhyme, reason, and rhythm

Please don't allow the work to take the best of you away from you. Allow the work to bring the best of you closer to you. Keep being who you are unconditionally, do the good work, do it like you are here to do it, and when you win, let the work take the glory but please come back home to yourself.

1. Learn to listen to your work, learn to take a pause, and learn to be with it, without trying to achieve something out of it.

2. If there is a goal, any goal at hand, any work that demands your attention, or any person who needs your concern, be the person that work needs you to be. Be the person who shows up.

3. You have to take your own sweet time while you are working. You have to allow your work to find its connection to your reality, you must not force it. You do that by pausing.

4. Always remember this while you are doing your work, the work is also building you up too. You both have an equal capacity to change each other. So give respect and take respect. If you made it till here, I can trust, that I don't have to teach you fairness.

5. Don't feed on your work for surviving day to day and let not your work feed on you. Maintain boundaries.

6. The good news is you don't have to figure it all out at once. Another piece of good news is you can fail and try again. You can take rest and try again. You can also save the battle for later if it's too much for your stride. You can seek help, learn how to improve, and try again. But you can always come back and see it through eye to eye and make it happen. It's a matter of choice. The work that has piled up over the years. The work that has already been done by someone else. The work that has been done and damaged. Everything can be put together. It's a matter of pure choice. You can do it now if you want to.

7. So, if there is something that you want to do and you are not able to do it, make peace with it. Because something in you isn't convinced to do it yet, its not the right time.

8. We don't always do the work just for the sake of doing it. We do the work for many reasons, and those reasons are myriad. Sometimes anger drives us, sometimes passion, sometimes sheer boredom. I don't know your reasons, but you know them well. If proving something to someone is your reason, then state it as it is; don't lie to yourself. You can't afford to lie to yourself.

9. Remember this: when you are pursuing a goal or protecting someone you love, you aren't fighting with anything outside of yourself. You are fighting with your own self. What is making you feel defeated? What is making you feel vulnerable? What is making you feel a little lost? What is making you feel distracted? What is making you unsafe? You must remember that the demons, the people, the stories—everything that is keeping you away from your happy, carefree self—is inside of you. You are fighting with them, and you are using your work to be free of them.

10. Most of the times you do the work to let go of outdated attitudes, patterns, path and integrate new ways of living.

11. So, keep that in mind, you are doing this work to make peace with your work, and make peace with everything that is keeping you away from your carefree self, happy soul.

12. The minute you made peace with your work, is the minute you start creating your dream to reality.

13. Keep the balance. Know when to give everything you've got and when to not move a finger. Know when to give just enough.

14. Be kind to yourself, trust yourself, trust the work you are doing, and wait and see for the work to evolve before you give more efforts, relax.

15. Also, take time to do your self work. So, that you can evolve and allow your work to expand.

16. The result of good work is always opportunity to do more good work.

17. Please do not push a person, a team, work , or a situation to change according to your will.

18. Allow them to grow and evolve quietly, silently, effortlessly in their own way. Force and pressure will never ignite their spirit.

19. Care for them, allow them to be, because some people come to life just to take some rest, understand the nature of work, before giving it a medicine, is the cure.

You have to wait and see

Ever heard someone say, "I won the battle, but I lost myself"? Trust me, you can't afford to say that. There is no work out there that asks you to sacrifice the real you. There is no person who truly loves you and wants you to be someone else.

You must use your focus and concentration in a controlled environment. Focus on places, people, and situations that are already in sync with you, the environments you already know, and the people who already trust you and are willing to invest in you.

When dealing with something beyond your control, working in uncharted territories, you must see more than you are capable of seeing and hear more than you are capable of hearing. For that, you need unconditional patience and intact self-awareness.

For one simple reason, you can't bond with wilderness; you can't control it. There are some situations you shouldn't dare to control. You need to be humble. You need to listen, see, stay in the moment, and wait.

While treading uncharted territories, the worst thing you can do is to focus solely on the work or on the person demanding your complete attention. You need to periodically shift your focus and ask yourself, "Am I losing myself in this person? Am I losing myself in this battle?"

Check if your inner world is intact, if your little spark is still alive, and if you are at peace with yourself. Stand in your own power, and be someone who isn't afraid to take the right advice, even if it comes from an enemy. Learn how to listen and observe because sometimes the medicine comes from the monster.

How do you do that?

1. Stay in the moment.
2. Quietly engage and actively disengage to rest.
3. Sit and wait for your turn.
4. Make a list of what is solving the problem and what is breaking the solution.
5. Spend time with yourself.
6. Observe everything and everyone.
7. Notice what naturally draws your attention.
8. Be safe, protect yourself, and learn to trust yourself.
9. Approach the work quietly, build trust, and then build momentum to collaborate.
10. When the work is done, let go; don't hold on to it.
11. Keep a check on the songs that find your way, the pictures you are taking, that's how you stay in touch with what you are feeling, whom you are paying attention to, and what you are dealing with.

Again, know when to give everything you've got and when to not even move a finger. What you cannot control, your little bliss will find a way through.

ONE LOVE

Stay rooted, committed, and sustain

So, once you know what you are up to—the goal at hand, the person in front of you, the challenge in front of you—invest your energy completely. Be selfless while doing so.

Before you take on a task or pick someone up, you have a choice. But once you commit to it, your only choice is to engage with it as selflessly as possible. You, as an individual, are the second person in the story. The first person will always be the person or the work you are actively engaging with. They will be the face of the narrative.

So, once you've made the choice to do the work:

1. Create your clauses and conditions.
2. Know and communicate your boundaries.
3. Try to have a map or direction to follow.
4. Know exactly what you want to achieve.
5. Be adaptable to changing seasons.

When you are committed to something, fear naturally takes a back seat. It's simple. Once you decide where to invest your work, you will start working at it. Your goal will be to keep your promises. You won't care as much about the outcome but rather how well you keep your promise.

As you remain committed to keeping your promises, the work at hand and the person in front of you will start to trust you in return. They will take care of you and sustain you. It's a very organic process of giving and receiving. Because they now trust you, no matter what happens, you will take one step forward to complete what you have started.

There will be setbacks, things that don't work out, discussions that don't align, rejections, and closed doors.

But if you make that promise, remain adaptable to the ever-changing environment, and stick to your boundaries, you will complete the work as promised. You will keep your promises without paying high cost.

Remember there is a season to introspect, there is a season to dream and plan, there is a season to work, a season to evaluate and take feedback, a season to celebrate and rest.

Your little bliss will help you to keep your promises without paying a high cost for it. So, if you allow it to take the lead. It's simple: pick the work, commit to it, adapt to the season, and complete everything you have started, but remember allow your little bliss to take the lead, I know you love to be in control, but allow the wind to change the directions a little bit.

Find your stride, stay your course

In the ever-expanding universe, everything finds its way to life; it's just a matter of time and space.

The work you have touched, the story you are writing, the wealth you are building, and the life you are living have all begun before they were brought into your reality for you to experience. They chose you before you chose them. They have their own worth, value, and evolution and they will help you to build your worth, value, and evolution accordingly.

So, the work you are doing, the person you are engaging with, the money you are investing—everything has its own value, its own story, a direction to go, and a destination to reach.

ONE LOVE

Your paths have crossed because you both are heading in the same direction, with the same intention, and towards the same destination. If you are thinking you are all alone, understand that you are not. There is an active dialogue, interaction, and silence between you and the work you are doing, the person you are engaging with, the environment, time, and space you are living in.

While you are giving your head, heart, and soul to the work or to that person, the person and the work will also interact with you with the same intensity. They are also living in an ever-expanding, exploring, and on their own journey. So, allow them to be whoever they want to be.

If you give enough freedom to the person and the work, they will show up and interact with you with the same freedom. If you give them enough space to settle, inspire them to find a better version of themselves, hold good intentions for them, and let them be who they are, they will do the same for you, then life will be an act of love, honour, and cherishing.

Just like you, the work, the person in front of you, the situation, and the environment know how to be still, how to follow, how to take the lead, and how to take the leap. So, change your positions accordingly and flow.

If you are actively engaging and disengaging, work and pause, work and play, work and rest you will benefit from the force of the universe and reach your destination effortlessly. Every work you are doing and every person you are meeting has their own personal story. Most of the time, our journey is about being seen, heard, and understood for who we are.

If you are trying hard to sustain yourself, you don't have to—the work you are doing will sustain you. Just do the work with everything that you are, and it will help you sustain.

∞

So, its okay to lose a grip on you, while following my path?

I said, yes, because you lost the grip on me and took a ride on whatever that came your way. That made me little free. I slept, overslept, dreamt, and found you in my dreams.

The girl looked thoughtful and asked, "So, once I lose the grip on you, a memory of you, and our good old days, all the times you came to my rescue and the stories we shared, I will be free?"

I responded gently, "Yes, you will be free. You will stop looking for me in a Bentley, a G63, or any of those symbols. You will see them for what they are. If you want to buy them, you will; if not, you will be okay without them."

She nodded, absorbing the words. "So, I will know how not to pay a high cost for everything I want to have?"

"Exactly," I confirmed. "You will simply be. When you can afford something, you will have it; otherwise, you will be free. You'll use the bike, the e-scooter if you want to, or you can simply walk."

She considered this, a small smile forming. "Because now I know how to take my power back, be comfortable with myself, and not force anything to happen?"

"That's right," I said. "You'll enjoy watching the boats in the ocean more than taking a ride on them. Then you will eventually lead to a dining on the sea. You'll understand that whatever is meant to come to you will always find its way, giving you good memories, making you smile from ear to ear, and making you feel precious and rare."

"So, I don't have to go out and look for people, places, and things to make me feel this way?" she asked.

"No," I reassured her. "You already know you are precious, special, and loved unconditionally. You have an inheritance of love that's endless. You will start seeing life for what it is, agreeing with where it takes you, appreciating it more, and appreciating people more. You'll see them for who they truly are."

She looked thoughtful again. "If I like what I see, I will care for it, tend to it, nurture it, and let it blossom?"

"Yes," I said. "And if you don't like it, you will let it go, turn away, because you now know how to avoid giving yourself to anything that makes you feel like you have to be something else other than yourself. You have a better view now, knowing where to see, what to look for, and what to give into."

As she absorbed my words, I knew that the journey we shared had given her the clarity to see and appreciate life in a new light, understanding her own value and power in ways she hadn't before.

She came close to me and said "Between you and me, I actually never thought I was paying a high cost for you. I thought you are very affordable, and you are mine already."

Smiles.

∞

CHAPTER 4
The Way to Your Heart

Help my eyes to see the best in people, help my ears to hear only good things, and help my heart to be kind and compassionate.

We all know the story, but I will tell it again.

Once, there was a little boy who loved to chase butterflies. He ran and ran, but he couldn't catch any. One day, tired from running, he sat down and relaxed. As he sat quietly, a butterfly gently landed right on the tip of his nose.

That's how it works. That's how the heart works. Relax so that your heart stops pushing and pulling, chasing and running.

Stay true to the moment you are in, feel safe within your own home, and love yourself for exactly who you are. If you do that, you will touch your own heart, and you will feel warm and comfortable.

Your heart will start speaking to you; it will make you draw, paint, cook, read, and play. It will make you smile.

Relax and just be.

You can relax, sing a song, talk a lot, and go to play

In between work, in between conversations, in between every activity, please relax a bit. Bring relaxation to every part of your body. Do not lose your connection to your body, mind, and soul. Relaxing, hugging, taking a nap, going for a walk, stretching, and listening to the birds' song.

If you can relax before you begin your work, relax while doing it, relax under pressure, and then go back to relaxation, know that you know how to take your power back.

Give yourself to everything that comes your way in the form of work, a person, or a relationship, and then take back your power, your spark, and return home to yourself.

When the purpose of the meeting is fulfilled, the goal is achieved, and the work is complete, take your power back by relaxing, resting, and rejuvenating.

Now, do not ask me how to relax because you know how to relax.

If you know how to relax, it means you already know how to get back to trying after failing, how to get back home after completing the work, and how to get back to work after success. People who can relax can stay humble, control their emotions, and know how to take back their power effortlessly.

Relaxation is the only medicine for pain, and when you are growing, evolving, and stretching your limits, pain visits you like a good friend. If you relax a little bit, it will help you find grace and glory in growth.

Gratitude

You know how to call people back to life. It's simple: by smiling, laughing, admiring, showing affection, and appreciating them.

You don't have to know a person to smile at them. You don't have to know someone to appreciate the work they are doing, the dress they are wearing, or even have a direct conversation with them.

You can actually look at people from a distance and appreciate the work they are doing, the person they are, the values they stand by, the promises they are keeping, and the fight they are keeping up with silently but consistently.

By appreciating, you are rewarding yourself with joy and bliss, and training yourself to see good in everything. By appreciating from a distance, you are sending them a spirit of goodwill to help them prosper and grow. By participating in celebrations and festivals, you are lifting your own spirit. By thanking them, you are affirming their value and their presence.

It's not when you win, but when you get appreciated by people who matters to you, for what you did, that's when you know your purpose is fulfilled.

Life force isn't something that is available everywhere in the universe. But by appreciating, you can actually bring a rock back to life. Gratitude is the most powerful tool given to us. By giving to the people who matter, you are increasing the life force within the existence of their lives, their value, and eventually the life force of this planet.

Say thank you, I love you, I forgive you, I miss you, I am you, and I am sorry.

Say it like you mean it.

Because some people come back to life just to be with you, just to stay with you; just to see you smile and laugh with you once more, you mean the world to them.

Celebrate festivals, give parades and serenades, cheer for their glory, chant for their success, and when you look into their eyes, smile at them everlastingly. So that they remember they are very much loved, and with that look in your eyes, they can stay forever appreciated.

That little deer is trying too hard, I sent it your way, so that you can sing a song, and it will know how to listen.

Empathy

Do you care enough? That is the question.

Wherever you are, whatever you are doing, whomever you are spending time with—do you care enough?

Do you care enough about yourself, the person standing in front of you in the mirror? Will you help yourself when needed? Will you take a step back from anything that is causing you pain? Will you help yourself take that leap and let go of everything that is holding you back? Do you care enough to ask for help when needed? Do you care enough to be the person your inner child wants you to be?

Empathy starts at home; compassion is internal work first. Take care of yourself, protect yourself, and create boundaries for yourself first. Please be your best friend.

Once that has been done, you will find yourself coming out of a victim mentality and standing out as a true human. If you know how to take care of yourself, you will naturally know how to take care of others.

The work you are doing, the relationships you have with others, will naturally transform into works of the heart. When you do it that way, the heart expands. The relationships and work will not just help you sustain but will attract many others who will join your journey and strengthen your hearts work.

If you know how to protect, guard, and see from the heart, you will always perform better than your ability. You will naturally have a Midas Touch, transforming every challenge into true prosperity and well-being. You will naturally become a leader. But remember a true leader know how to love themselves first. Once that is done, people who need help will come and ask you to lead.

Now, I am not asking you to go out of your way to give your compassion to everyone who stops by. But recognize who truly needs your help, if you are in a position to help, do your job. Give help.

Extend your help as much as you can. You don't have to go beyond your limitations. You can help as much as you can and let the rest be taken care of by someone else. Now and then, strangers come and ask for help. If you can recognize that they truly need it, extend your hand without questioning.

The ten-dollar bill you give to feed someone hungry might cause a small argument between you and your fiancé. You might judge him, and you might even leave him. You might search for a better job, meet your person who sees your value, and makes you feel it's okay to be kind. They might encourage you to do something that not only helps you but also others, leading you to success, wealth, and a fulfilled life with the love of your life. Life works in mysterious ways.

Not everyone who comes to your doorstep is asking for your help; some might actually come to help you. You might feed them, give them a small amount of money, or offer them clothes, but in return, they might give you a blessing to stay blessed, protected, and taken care of. A blessing in exchange for a ten-dollar bill is worth more than that dress you bought from a store just to wear for the summer.

If you have the capacity to give from your heart, see from your heart, and listen to your heart, then everything you do will have value. Everything you touch will become a treasure on the trail. If you can hold empathy in your heart, the entire universe—plants, trees, birds, stones—will recognize you by your heart. You will be safe. They will make you smile, make you feel safe, and there will always be a friend in every room you enter. They will tell you good stories and guide you to your true destiny.

Please remember this: don't ever close your heart. If you do, you will not be able to see the beauty of this life. Your heart's way is the gateway to many sources of knowledge, wealth, wisdom, love, friends, and family. Keep it open; let it stay open. If people close doors in your face, let them. But remember, let them never close your heart.

Your heart will always know the way through. People who take insights from their hearts naturally go to the right place at the right time. They truly do. The only work you have to do is to avoid indulging in what could have been or what you might have had.

Refuge permission to anyone who hooks you or bait you by your longings and desires. Then you will never get lost. Simple, humble, and self-sufficient people are special. They always smile, always win in the end, and will always have a home and someone to love. It's the truth.

Grief

It would be so wrong if we don't give a moment to our sorrow, loss, and grief. Let your heart take its sweet time in between experiences to feel what is has to feel.

Salt water heals, let tears flow effortlessly. Be gentle with yourself. If you feel like crying please cry. Tears, rain, river, ocean, they are all same, please cry, and be kind to your heart, please be vulnerable. Its okay. People who love you will see through your pain, your vulnerability, they have space to hold tears from your eyes. Distance doesn't matter, oceans apart, your pain can reach heart to heart, if you give yourself a moment to feel, know that, you will have someone to heal, you aren't alone in your pain, you will heal.

Every cry is heard. This universe is a friendly place to be. You can always count on all your well-wishers plus one. There is always a friend you didn't meet, someone who can listen to you from distance with out a memory of knowing you or meeting you ever in a lifetime. So, do not be afraid to be vulnerable and give into grief, when you have to. You have many friends some visible but many invisible. They will hold space for you every time you grieve.

Only by giving a moment into your grief, you will realize, that you are holding on to pain. Once you realize the pain is within you, you will see what you can do with it too.

∞

"How I wish I could share everything we were to everyone I know, and how special you are to me. I want say it to my friends, family, every stranger I meet and greet. If they don't know you like I know you, I don't want to be their friends, I don't want to talk to them, or share with them. I fear no one would believe me. Finding bliss in a vessel of wheels?" she mused.

"I had that fear too," I replied gently. "Forget about everyone else. I worried that if I shared what I am with you, you might run away from me, choosing to leave me behind."

"I knew it from the day we met," I continued. "I knew you more than you knew yourself."

"But remember to do yourself a favour and share it with no one. The more you talk about our story—the vessel with wheels and the bag of flesh and bones—the more we trap ourselves, isolating each other, and distancing ourselves from who we truly are."

"I cannot always remain a vessel of wheels, and you cannot remain just a bag of flesh and bones."

"We are here to free each other from any traps, plots, memories, or songs. We cannot confine ourselves to a cage."

"Our purpose is to allow the eternal state of bliss and to share that bliss with the world."

"The more you lean in and allow the state of bliss to lead, the more you'll share what bliss is all about. That's when we truly become free."

"You needn't worry about the plots, stories, and songs."

"As long as you are lead by your bliss, others will naturally sense it. Those who remain in bliss will understand you without needing words. People will recognize your true self and, through you, they'll come to know me as well. They'll see the beauty in us, like each others work of art, and they will know what we seek is sacred, innocence, and pure."

"But the moment you try to force them to see eternity within a story or a plot, a song, or a vessel with wheels, they'll turn away. No one wants to be confined by a story; everyone seeks freedom."

Everyone wants to be little free, than they were yesterday, including you and me, we come together to set us free.

"You understand this better than anyone. The beauty lies in remaining in the eternal state of bliss, **sat-chit-anandha**."

∞

CHAPTER 5
Come as You Are

Once upon a time, there was a little duckling who looked a bit different from the others. The other animals in the barnyard called it "ugly." This made the duckling feel very sad. It often wandered by itself, feeling lonely and misunderstood.

As the seasons changed, the little duckling grew older and bigger and became a graceful swan!

The swan felt so happy and proud of its new self. Now, everyone admired its beauty and grace. The swan realized that it didn't matter what others had said before. It had grown into something special and found its true place in the world. And from then on, it lived happily ever after.

Say the words, make the move, take your position, and be who you are supposed to be. As humans, we play different roles; every role demands a different version of us, and every human wants something that only you can provide.

So, it's very natural that we walk into the world and play the role of what is expected of us, what is demanded of us, and what is right for the structure and environment we are living in.

It's also true that not everybody deserves or derives the best of you. Not many can find a way to your heart. Not many can see you for who you are. Not many can understand your silence, and not many can understand your language and words. How many of us have failed to win back someone with an explanation?

So, the experience of life naturally leads us to privacy. Be a little cautious about what to share and how much to share. The world runs on curiosity, judgments, and mostly gossip. To walk into a room and be who you truly are is almost a risk. But are you willing to take that risk?

If you are, let's find a simple and sustainable solution to the so-called "come as you are" concept:

1. Communicate your intentions before you communicate your story. Despite your imperfections, you can still get the job done by focusing on the job. If you have done enough work to sustain and if you really care about what you do, you just have to be honest about it.

2. You have a spine, an antenna to the cosmos; you can rely on it. It makes you self-reliant. Your spine is the true source for your wings to grow.

3. Use more than your words, use more than your eyes; use your body language to set your boundaries and protect your space.

4. Wake up your body, mind, and soul before you enter into your day. At the end of the day, wherever you go to visit or whomever you have spent time with, take back your power and come back home to yourself.

5. In every room you enter, there is a spot for you. Find that spot and stay there for a moment before you move into the room. Move where you are naturally drawn to.

6. Every good conversation starts by listening. Every good speech starts after taking a moment with yourself.

7. You don't have to force connections. See who naturally comes to you without much asking. Yes, there are people who give you that look to make you feel less about yourself. All you have to do is turn your head and look for a better view. We live in a big world with all kinds of people. We just have to find our kind of people.

8. If someone is actively taking away your energy, walk with that person into an open space or nature. Look out for energy hunters—people who want to hook you up with your longings and desires. Stay away from them; run away from them. Do not let them come for your soul. If there isn't enough give-and-take in a conversation, limit the conversation.

9. There are people who need your attention, your validation, your affection, your time, your energy, and your space. But only you have the choice. Be selfish with your choices and selfless with your commitments.

10. Noise cancellation works. Tune into your inner world before you sing your song.

11. In intimate meetings, when you feel a longing for the person in front of your eyes, try to avoid eye contact. You can only be vulnerable with someone who makes you feel free and safe.

12. Do not participate in one-on-one meetings with someone you aren't comfortable with. Correct people who are trying to mislead. You must, kindly do so. Don't overlook bad behaviour and disrespectful conversations. Don't forgive people before they apologize. If they are asking for another explanation and another, are you with the right person?

"Come as you are" comes with many clauses and conditions. When I say "come as you are," it means rely on your spine, rely on your intuition, rely on the work you have done, and rely on what you unconditionally care about, and then be honest about it with people, places, and situations. Not many people have the right to choose their audience, but if you have a choice, choose the right ones.

Share and withhold

If you can maintain a beautiful synchronicity between what you share and what you withhold, you can actually save yourself.

Here are a few things to share:

1. The journey you have had will always have a roadmap; please share it with the world. The knowledge that you have acquired, the wisdom that you have gained, and the results that you have achieved—give them back to the world. Always share the source of the information, inspiration, and dreams that have been fulfilled for you with this world. The work that is completed—please give it to the world.

2. Share the fruits of your labor with only those who truly care about you.

3. If you have an opportunity to give solace to someone's grief, please share the part of you that has endured that kind of grief, but only with those who need to hear it, to let them know they aren't alone.

4. See where you obtained your resources from and give back to the same places with your work, vision, and contribution of resources. We all have our own trials with life—something that we escaped by pure grace or resources that came very naturally to us. Find similar causes and give back. It is very important to choose the right causes.

Here are a few things to withhold:

1. Share your personal story only with people who truly care about you and who need to hear it. Keep your plans, insights, and dreams to yourself until they come true. Protect your journal, your belongings, and your memories.

2. Be silent until the work is completed, the results are here, and the people who care about you accept, appreciate, celebrate, and acknowledge your efforts. Keep the fruits of your labor to yourself, share them only with family and friends who have seen you through the journey without making you feel alone.

3. Protect your space, time, and energy. By all means, protect your gifts, your light, your vision, and your strengths and weaknesses.

4. Keep your mistakes to yourself; share them only with people who truly understand and with those who need to unburden themselves from their own mistakes.

5. You must have compassion, but be careful about your charity. Pick causes that resonate and align with your journey. Empathy is precious; you cannot give it to just anyone who comes your way. Some people may try to pull you out of your goodwill. So, don't offer help to just anybody. Use discernment, please.

∞

"I am still afraid," she said, her voice trembling. "I've been with you all along. We shared drives in the nights and early morning dew. We rescued sparrows, sung songs, laughed our hearts out and loud, talked to our friends for hours, went to places only we knew, carried flowers and vegetables from markets, and spotted

all dangers in sight. You know all my stories by heart, and now you're asking me to leave behind everything I ever was with you and find something new."

"I'm afraid to walk in the darkness," she continued. "How will I protect myself from predators? Since you came into my life, many people have stepped back. They see in me what you see in me."

"You've given me the rear view, shown me my blind spots, given me directions, and helped me navigate the world with awareness. You've taken me to destinations, provided beautiful views, and always made me feel special and precious."

"There have been so many laughs, songs, tricks, shortcuts, and countless moments calling to eternity. I'm afraid of losing you. I don't know anything that can replace you. Are you planning on leaving me all alone, all by myself?"

"Not really," I said gently. "You didn't quite get it, did you?"

"I am yours, and you have me. I will keep my promises. I will take you home, safe to your parents, and then further to the beyond. I will change your directions, be your map, and be the light in the dark. I am the heart of the city you live in. If you have to climb a mountain, I will be a stepping stone. In every forest you walk through, in every ocean you dive into, I will draw a path with glittering stars and gold, just as I've done before."

"If you still feel lonely, just ask yourself what I would do if I were there with you. You'll find your answer. I pray that one day you don't need to ask that question because you are already in Sat Chit Ananda, without needing me. Until then, if you sit in the dark, I will show up as stars. If you keep looking at stars, I will appear as sunshine. Every time you leap, I will give you wings. Every time you fall, I will catch you in my arms. If you find yourself in galaxies, I will be your starship. If you want to take a flight, I will be your jet.

If you want to run a mile, I will be your shoes. Wherever you want to go, I will be your guide, your light. One step ahead, so you can see better."

"You can trust me; I have your itinerary. I know all your stops, your destinations, the people you need to meet and make amends with, and those you need to celebrate with. I know the way home. I will never lose you or leave you in darkness. I will always lead you to the light, through the good and the bad, using everything in sight, always in the best interest of everything due, dew, and true. Focus on the light and the pure white, and let go of the dark and the black."

"But what if I have to lose you to someone else?" she asked. "I don't have it in me to replace you with another vessel with wheels. What if they don't take care of you like I do? What if I miss recognizing you in another cycle of life?"

"Look into the mirror," I said quietly.

She looked.

"Who do you look like?" I asked.

"They say I look like my aunt, my dad's beloved sister."

"Now, don't you think you were recycled and reinvented?" I continued.

"Do you really think your dad loves you because you have a face that reflects his DNA? He loves you more than that—not for what you look like, but for who you are to him—a source of love, joy, and bliss. Just as you have been to me, endlessly and unconditionally."

I reminded her again "You will always know me without knowing me. You will always find me without searching for me. We will cherish each other without having a memory of knowing each-other. We come together so gently, so dearly, to love, honour, and cherish for whatever journey we have to take, for a minute or many."

She looked away, and I look wherever she looks to give her a better view.

∞

CHAPTER 6
Let's See How The Cosmos Work

So - Hum: I am that

Once upon a time, there was a special bull named Nandhi. Nandhi loved Lord Siva, who was a kind and powerful god.

Nandhi was very happy just sitting quietly in front of Lord Siva every day. Anyone who wanted to talk to Lord Siva had to go through Nandhi first because he was the guardian.

Nandhi always saw the good in everyone and helped them find their best way to Lord Siva. Each time he helped someone, Nandhi felt closer to Lord Siva and learned more about him.

Because he loved Lord Siva so much, Nandhi found his sat-chit-ananda—true joy and peace—in being close to him.

So, remember Nandhi's story. When you stay happy and notice the good things around you, you can help others find their own sat-chit-ananda too. By seeing the best in people and guiding them, you help make the world a better place.

Our faith will be tested

If there is a way to the heart of the cosmos, it is through your faith. The cosmos, universe, or the intelligence of the universe qualifies you by your faith.

What is your capacity to trust life, for what it already is?

I am right now contemplating to understand and reflect: "If you have faith in yourself that is truly divine in nature, if there isn't something that isn't in the universe, it shall be created for you. "- Swami Yukteswar

What is that we desire so much that the universe itself agrees to create it just because we asked?

The ones who have the potential to hold good faith are the ones who sees good, the ones who sees bad, and then recognizes its purpose.

Now, if you look at the boulders falling from the mountain, which have the ability to crush your head and many others in the village, the ones who are built in faith know how to direct them to a river and create a lake with them. You may ask how?

Faith doesn't judge anything as good or bad. Faith sees things that you cannot see, listens to what you cannot hear, and does what you naturally would not choose to do. The ones who transform catastrophes into blessings in disguise are those who are built in faith. The easiest way to be in faith is to understand its happening for a reason.

People of faith know their seasons. They know how to introspect, how to start something new, make something out of nothing, evaluate, take feedback, and then take their power back. They are with themselves, they rest, and relax.

They don't validate themselves with haves and have nots, they don't gather insecurities or securities by holding on to something because they know they are being taken care of equally on their sad days and happy days. They understand they are in the moment for a reason; they know their values, their breakthroughs, and they are ready to fall or fly into grace.

People of faith do not bend to other people's opinions, challenging circumstances, or human attachments. They rise above it and see things from a bird's point of view. At any given point, people who have faith will rise above the situation, person, or challenge in front of them and see what is the best they can make out of it for the journey forward.

The power of faith is simple and accurate. It can move mountains for you, make a mountain out of a mud hill, and carry the entire mountain on a little finger for you.

During tough times:

1. Try to find a quote that speaks safety to your heart and hold on to it.
2. Try waking up to a sunrise or set some time to see the sunset.
3. Try sleeping outdoors and watching the stars.
4. Do not judge any experience as good or bad.
5. Don't run away; don't try to catch up.
6. Always know there is more than what you know.

In the ever-expanding universe, there is not one particle that feels left out or wasted; everything is intricate and falls into design. We can get a glimpse of the cosmos in everything we seek if only we have eyes to see.

When you focus on:

- Detoxing your body, mind, and spirit.
- Committing yourself to increase your capacity to unlearn and learn.
- Holding good intentions.
- Staying in gratitude.

You will naturally receive:

1. Insights and ideas.
2. Practices to sustain your ideas.
3. Tremendous willpower.
4. The ability to work, sustain, evolve, and transform the work.
5. The ability to make things happen and produce favourable and gratifying results for everyone involved.

Fame, fortune, speech, memory, beauty, intelligence, innocence, poetry, patience, faith, all has one source, that source is pure, and by being in *sat-chith-anadha* you can have access to everything there is in creation depending on the work you are doing and your intention behind it.

So, relax, then commit to what you care about, and flourish super naturally :).

Remember good company, good work, and good habits. When you touch the dark you can see the depth but you must bounce back to light. It is your right.

ONE LOVE

When the nature of connection itself is unconditional

When the nature of your connection with life itself is unconditional, no matter what happens with the work you are putting in, the person you love dearly, or the life you are living, you will always find yourself with them in a better time and place than where you began.

A connection with work, a person, or a place will find you time and again to be of your benefit. The connection may visit you for a season, a purpose, or a lifetime, but it is always meant to be of your benefit and to help you move forward and to remind you what is love all about.

So, if you have an unconditional connection with the life force, the work you are doing, or the person you are in love with, you do not need to feel sad when it goes away. You just have to trust that it will find its way back to you. If there is something in your life that you are dearly holding on to, instead of clinging to it, please, by all means, set it free.

Because when you let go, you allow the connection you have with the person to transform and expand, and it will find you again and again with every new evolution, new zeal, and freshness. Just like eagles that leap and fall, cartwheeling but never losing sight of each other, do not be afraid to let go, it will come your way anyway.

When you need to actively disengage from a group of people, a project, some work you are doing, or a person, understand that the next time you meet, you will recognize each other and give each other exactly what you both deserve, and that too unconditionally.

There is a time and place to receive the fruit of your labor. You don't have to overstep, cut through the crowd, or hold back. You can simply follow your path, and it will find you in its own way. People who follow their path knows it well, there is never a competition. We come to this planet to pay off our debts while contributing to the new world and joyfully receive our blessings in disguise.

So, if you didn't stay in a house long enough to reap the fruits of a tree you planted, you will go to a place where the harvest is ready. Everything finds its time and place, and every wish of yours will come true.

One way or another, you will always have what you invest in.

We don't know who created our world

Let's count five blessings every human has: air, water, sunlight, space, and ground. Who created these for us? Who made rainbows for us?

We all know, or are aware, that there is something beyond our gaze creating and holding it all together for us, just so we can live a lifetime here on earth.

As humans, we want to know. We have math to simplify, science to preserve, social structures to create culture, and community, art to reflect, language to express, and politics to define governance and leadership. But we all know from our experience that we still have a very limited vision.

People who perceive this universe as magical are very simple people, they just believe in god, they believe in his creation, they believe that the sun, moon, stars, oceans, and rainbows are reflections of that which is beyond everything.

Dreamers, scientists, may believe in aliens, travellers from other worlds, treasure cities, and unlimited resources, all hidden to be found. There is also talk of time travellers, gateways to other worlds, portals to different dimensions of reality, and new worlds. Even mothers act as a gateway for children to appear.

Now, my intention is not to push you to see something that you cannot see, but to accept that there is something we cannot see. Just as the sun, moon, and stars show up and embody magic, you can also show up and embody the same magic that made us part of this world.

Every single day, know that something is taking care of you. There is something you can bring into this world too—be a reflection of something that makes you feel magical. Take good care of what you are doing, how you are doing it, and who you are.

When you are in a position of power to take care of someone, do not shy away from being who you are. I believe the universe will find a way to take care of everyone you consider yourself responsible for through you. Believe it. Just as the sun is aging and burning, the cosmos is also using you to create value in this world while you last.

I pray everyday that what lasts of me, you, and everyone of us is bright, beloved, and blissful in every way.

CHAPTER 7
Who am I?

The question just makes you uncomfortable because it surpasses human potential; at least, that's how it makes us feel.

Our education doesn't help, the knowledge we acquire does not help, and the story we are living, the job we are doing—none of these mere facts about our existence help to answer this question.

The only way to answer this question, in the words of Ramana Maharishi, is by practicing self-inquiry.

Just ask this question with a genuine intention to know; that's all any true master asks you to do. That's the only work where we actually reach a focal point, where we truly intend to ask: Who am I?

I always resisted asking this question. It was almost as if I was afraid to face myself, as if I knew the story I was living, the people I love, the work I was doing—those were my boundaries. I belonged here; I was good as I was. I didn't want to know more; I was truly fine, self-sufficient. I didn't want to know more than that.

But now, I at least understand why people ask that question.

Now, you may ask, why should I question? What is the need for it? Keep life very simple. Love what you love and get to work.

We all know that even by doing an excellent job of attracting everything we want, we still end up wanting more than what we already have and feeling a little less than how we want to feel.

Even after putting on the greatest show of our lives out there in this world, someone can still make us feel a little insignificant. It doesn't take much—just one look in the eye to make us feel a little less than what we are.

If it's from a stranger who gives us that look, we can live with that; it only hurts a little. Over time, we will also learn to look away and even roll our eyes a little bit to overcome it.

If it's from someone we love and care about, it hurts a little more—a rejection. We try to change for the better; we call it self-growth.

But if that someone is not just someone we love but the reason we exist, that's when we crumble, we fall apart, and the process that brings us back to life is our transformation.

Oftentimes, when we find what we love, our purpose, we don't just give what we've got; we become what it needs us to be.

Because loving this person, living this dream, and building this vision is our life's work, the very reason we thought we had our prāna, the life force, the simple breath we take.

Endings or rejections from what we love cannot be just another closed door. A simple change of personality will not suffice, nor will knocking on other doors fix it for us.

It feels like someone took something away from us—a part of us, our purpose, a reason to accept life for what it is.

That's when we actually feel helpless. That's when we call upon death while we are living. That's when the caterpillar goes into a cocoon, and the only way it can return to the world is by transforming into a butterfly.

If not for this, what am I here for? Who am I supposed to be? I can't go back to who I was, nor do I know where to go.

If we decide to question, we will question everything—our entire existence. But we must question. The first step to self-love and self-care is introspection and reflection. By asking a question, we move towards an answer. The question is very simple: Who am I?

Sages say this question leads us to our true destiny and sets our path towards our eternal home. They suggest not to be afraid to see yourself for who you are.

The world discovered by the butterfly is very different from the world the caterpillar lived in.

The good news is you don't have to do anything to change your world; nature itself picks you out of a pond and drops you into the ocean.

Take life for what it is, a little less grumpy and more chill. Pose this question in your quiet moments, when you are with yourself, when you are meditating, while looking at a sunrise, or on a walk. Ask with the intention to know.

To give a little more hype. Remember that person who tried to make you feel like just another fish in their pond? Well, now look them straight in the eye and tell them, "I ain't just another fish in your little pond—damn it, I am the entire ocean!"

And don't say it for the sake of an attitude— say it because you know it's the truth. That's a real deal. That's freedom. Freedom in knowing the truth. That's where true joy comes form.

We all deserve to know the truth. We all deserve to be in joy. We all deserve to just be.

P.S : This little bubble of love we live in is everything that we ever need. But now and then a humming bird comes our way and asks, why do you put yourself in a cage? Come with me, there is a beautiful world out there, and you can fly too.

∞

Beloved,

We have been there all along, traveled long and far, and done it all—not once, not twice, but many, many times. We have lived the same song. I have been with you all along. I once was a Bentley, a horse, a jet, a peacock, a train, an elephant—everything you are spotting again. I am not someone new; I am somebody you always knew.

It's time to embrace the little light. Leave behind everything that pulls you back into darkness.

I came to change the songs you are listening, change the direction you are leading into. Step out of your carousel, merry go arounds. You have been there, done that, endless conversations that is keeping you out of your endless possibilities.

ONE LOVE

I came to give you a taste of how beautiful silence can be, if you allow it to be.

No song can pull you out of your misery, but your sweet silence can.

No amount of money can fill your vault, but your gratitude can.

Stop walking like a beggar, your heart can pull treasures out of every trial.

It breaks my heart to see you searching for love in all the wrong places, while you are leading love itself to everything you touch, see, and speak to.

You aren't here to keep regrets, you are here to celebrate every new joy everlastingly so.

I am here. So are you. We cannot return to who we once were, but we can guide each other back to the light. We have an inheritance of love, and it will sustain us through.

Raise up to the Sovereign. Let the Sun emerge from its shades. Let your small ponds lead you to the ocean. Birds are singing, lotuses are blossoming. Once in a blue moon, we meet by serendipity. Every time we meet, it is the same game: I look at you, and you look away. You look at me, and I look away.

The Moon whispers to the Sun, "I've been up waiting all night just to see you smile, and now I can fade into your smile."

As if we cannot afford each other. As if we are not good enough for each other. Beloved, listen to me: it has always been this way. We cannot afford to lose each other to another cycle of life and death. We are one love.

"Remember this you out of everyone can leave me for a moment or many. But you cannot afford to loose our path to love, eternity, our sweet home."

It's time for you to see your own light. It's time to be a champion of change. Initiate change. Make magic out of your mess. We have an inheritance of love; you are loved more than you know and more, by me and an endless universe.

Step up, step out, be fearless, and face the Golden Sun. You are healthy, happy, and wealthy. You will be given the resources you need, the people you require, and the good work you seek. There is so much good work for a beautiful world to emerge and so much love to be shared through our inheritance of love. If you lead with love, angels will visit you every other day.

Baby you have a better view of the ocean of eternity than I have; But if you don't see it, if you don't go there often, if you aren't going in that direction. I am going there anyway, and I will lead you there anyway. But if you go there first, I will be there soon. Please, try and be one step ahead of me, like always. So, that when I come home, you are already there in sat-chit-anadha.

You have been running in those shoes for so long; they are old, worn out, and dirty. I have picked you up in my car many times. Neither I nor you deserve to be apart. The wheels of my vessel and the flesh and bones of your being are meant to move in the direction of the light. When we come together, we are one with everything there is.

So, allow the truth to come in, allow the awareness to come in, allow the bliss to come in.

Whatever way if finds you, I hope you recognize it, just like you recognized me.

Come home baby, wherever you were lead by your light, I will be there, in sunshine, and rainbows, little rain drizzle, moon light, billion stars, locking deer eyes with head lights to see you smile. Once more and forever.

ONE LOVE

Love, laughter, life, memories, and timeless moments; we don't have to steal what is rightfully ours to share; If we follow our path one way or infinite ways we are bound to come back home to each other.

—

Here's the keys, that I kept so dearly to my heart to yours. You are rare, precious, something of value, so special, to me, and an endless universe I got to see through you.

I am now giving you permission to go above and beyond me and be eternally free.

∞

Note from the Author

Here are some quotes that helped me to hold on to my little light

1. Sri Krishna: "The only way you can conquer me is through love, there I am gladly conquered."

2. Office and Bible: "Love is patient and kind; love does not envy or boast; it is not arrogant or rude. It does not insist on its own way; it is not irritable or resentful; it does not rejoice at wrongdoing, but rejoices with the truth."

3. Swami Vivekananda: "Don't look back—forward, infinite energy, infinite enthusiasm, infinite daring, and infinite patience—then alone can great deeds be accomplished."

4. Jiddu Krishnamurthy: "When you find love in wrong places, do nothing about it."

5. Unknown: "She has found the secret: When you stop seeking the artificial entertainment created by thoughts and words, the universe resumes the original entertainment. Birds, stars, clouds etc. come and dance before her and make her feel like the queen of the universe."

6. Paulo Coelho: "And, when you want something, all the universe conspires in helping you to achieve it."

7. Unknown: Love appears as relationship, but begins in solitude.

8. Babaji: If you give yourself what you need you have everything.

16.57 N - 80.50 E

I am from India (in-dee-uh). My mother tongue is Telugu (teh-luh-goo). We call Mother as Amma (a-mma), Father as Nana (nā-nā), and teacher as Guru (goo-roo).

Back home, we consider and trust these three people to lay our foundational principles to live the destiny we intend to live in this life. It means that wherever our soul came from, the minute we land into their hands and feet, they will help us to see better than we have seen up until now. They help us to bring forth a newly emerging life from within us. They stand firm whenever we want to revert to our old patterns and paths, help us meet the people with whom we need to make amends, and lovingly direct us towards our new, promising destiny by changing us for good and calling us to our new destiny.

I am one of those blessed souls who received this guidance from my Amma, Nana, and Guru. I am extremely thankful and grateful for their patience while I was on my path to self-discovery and answering my purpose.

I am eternally grateful.

So, I want to say something sweet in the language I know by heart. Telugu is poetic, simple, and sweet. It is the easiest language to learn and speak. I read my first poem, written by Sri Sri, in Telugu.

ONE LOVE

In Telugu, love means Prema (prai-maa), ego means Aham (ahaṁ), intellect means Buddi (buːdi), and life means Prana (prāna). These are only tools given to any human. How we use them and what we use them for are what lasts of us when we leave this place.

I hope everyone uses these tools for something good, to create something new so that the world will become a better place to live, and heaven will come closer to home. One day, in the face of an emerging new sun, everyone will say she comes from earth (Bhūmi), the place where everyone is of joy (ānandaṁ).

People of earth, we have the potential. Infinity is ∞.

You Don't Really Have to Read This

At the beginning of 2024, I was sitting in a coffee shop, looking at a blog I had written. I felt like there was more to it than what I had originally put down, even though I didn't quite know what that "more" was. For the first time, I sensed that there was something beyond what I was trying to express.

I casually asked AI, "Do you think this blog has the potential to be a book?" It said yes and shared some insights on how my blog could expand into a book. I told I wasn't ready and didn't have the energy to write a whole book, but the AI offered to help me with editing, chapter by chapter. That sealed the deal for me—the idea that my blog could actually become a book started to feel real.

But how could I see beyond what I had already written? How could I uncover what was missing? What am I not seeing?

Then I discovered Swami Rama on YouTube and started listening to his talks. I realized there were parallels between what I wanted to say and what he was saying. If any other spiritual teacher had told me to meditate, I probably would have refused. I didn't feel like sitting with myself back then. But Swami Rama was different; he had a playful humour about him. He shared stories about persuading his master to teach him superpowers, how he frightened a tiger, and he talked about his master with the innocence and affection of a child. Listening to him, I found myself wishing I could have met him, wish I had with him, what he had with his master.

I've been meditating for a decade, but Swami Rama was the first person who made me feel like wisdom could also be approachable and fun. His words and humour worked on me, and I found myself meditating again. Somehow, this inspired me, and I found 21,000 more words to turn my blog into a book in just two weeks.

It took two significant life experiences, to express myself in 1000 words after clearly looking at all the facts and observations of months to incorporate into a blog. And it took two weeks to stretch the blog into a book with 22,000 words and more.

How is that possible?

Its possible because I was aware that there is something more to what I am already seeing and I made my efforts, I meditated.

Meditation isn't the only solution. But it is one of many. Answers come in silence. Judgments come with loud voices.

I've never really liked writing. At the end of my studies, my engineering mindset convinced me that I was good at research. I convinced myself that maybe I could make friends through writing. You know, long-distance friendships. The few books I had read made me realize that I could fill a book with words. I mean, five different answers for one question and drawing parallels between them. How easy is that?

Throughout my entire academic life, I had my mom do my notes. My dad has terrible handwriting, but I even put him to work on bits and pieces. I photocopied my professors' notes to prepare for exams. I'd quickly calculate math answers and shout them out so I wouldn't have to write anything down. All my journals were empty, filled only with chocolate wrappers, silly wish lists, and little complaints. I avoided writing in every way, even in my examinations, I never wrote more than what is needed for me to get away with my life.

I do have a good handwriting. It depends on my mood. But if someone pushed me to read and write the whole paper, I can simply imitate my dad's terrible handwriting.

But, I have grown up now and I decided to become a writer.

I mean, me? A writer?

The universe does have a sense of humour—and God's jokes are really funny.

I jumped into the world of books without even knowing where it was leading me while keeping my career on the sidelines. I refused every person and every job that had the potential to take me away from writing. Even in its absence, I didn't allow anything to come my way that could potentially take me away from writing. I know when the words come I will have no choice but to surrender. I know I connect to something pure and unconditional here.

I am not really sure where this is taking me, but it feels like home. I held on to writing with all my heart, never forcing anything out of it or commanding it to be a certain way, or trying to achieve something out of it. I simply kept writing. I still wonder, is this really my language? Are these really my words? I try to relate as much as I can. When I fail to understand what I write, I move on to next.

I began watching films and reading books to understand and empathize with different stories. I read many books, two to three a week, thinking that someday I would know it all.

I learned that good poetry needs good metaphors, and to write compelling articles, you start by asking better questions and solving them step by step. To write a fairy tale, you have to change a person through a breathtaking experience. The simpler the conflict, the more drama we get into. To think differently, you have to read various subjects and the autobiographies of people who love those subjects and the subjects they love to read. I love research—give me a topic, and I'll dive into it and figure it all out. I mean, give me something, and I will figure everything out. That was my motto. I was writing randomly, never taking a minute to see what I was actually writing. For me, it was just a puzzle board; as long as it had a rhyme, I did not need a reason to write.

I still remember one of my cousin freaking out after reading my first book. Please tell me what happened to you. Honestly, I don't even know how I came up with that story—I was just searching for words, rhymes, and fancy titles for my new chapters, trying to figure out what the story was all about while imitating my favourite authors. Before I know there is a book in my hands, I was lost into words, structure, tone, and language. Editing and adding more mistakes. I missed the true essence of seeing the story for what it is. My very first attempt at self expression made me run back to my corporate job. Behave as if poetry never happened to me. I killed and paused my instinct to read by spending time in nature, watching animation, Disney, national geography, listening to audible, and reading only intellectually stimulating content, leading me further to anxiety, eventually back to nature, spirituality, and silence.

One day, I happened to read Shirdi Sai Baba's "Sai Satcharitra." It says, "Why do you think folklore songs sound so sweet? Why does everyone sing along when women in villages sing? Do you think they went to college? What kind of degree do they have? Do you really think they are intellectuals? They sing sweetly because they sing from their hearts." That was my "humbling" moment—my caterpillar moment. So, I decided to take a step back and see if I could write something from my heart itself when I am ready.

I did have a fear: what if everybody could see through me? I asked God for some wisdom, and wisdom has its own voice, and it spoke: Well, first try to figure out who you are, then if someone tries to look into you, they will only find me. How?, I have to write another book may be. But that's the deal we made. That gave me a little courage to be vulnerable in my own way.

Writing came back to my life very gently. Didn't allow me to get distorted but picked me up and gave me back to myself.

Even though my heart tells me I don't like writing, it also tells me that I'm good at finding the right words and putting them together. Writing helps me slow down my thoughts and guides me toward what I love, and through them, it gives me a way to love itself. So, it makes sense. I don't always know what I'm writing or what the story is, but that's okay. The books I wrote, the little poetry in my catalog, never really made sense to me until they shown me the mirror and asked me to see again once more. It took me years to actually listen to the work I wrote. I still feel like a little fool for not taking a moment to see what I actually wrote. The moment I found a chapter, I would move on to the next. The moment I wrote a poem, I would move on to the next. I lost a lot of drafts, never read my books, because the writer in me is leading me to a life different from what the reader in me is trying to understand. Different dimensions.

So, how do you see it? How do you see your own work?

By knowing that there's always more than what we see, we allow the awareness to come in.

That's transformation. The butterfly effect. When you make an effort to know, you will know what you need to know. You don't have to know it all, but you need to know what you need to know. You don't have to listen to everybody, including me; you can just listen to your heart—it has something to say, actually, so much to say. Heart needs your vulnerability.

When you find what you love, don't try to make it fit into what you already know. Allow it to reveal itself, and allow it to find its own way to love itself. Your job doesn't end when you find what you love; it continues as what you love finds its way to love itself. Be a guide, not a dictator.

Sometimes, finding love aligns you on the same path, but often, everything has its own way of finding love. Just because you've met someone or found something you love doesn't mean you own them. It means you've found them on your way to love, and by some good fortune, you've awakened that love within them, we call it a connection, and we make promises, just in case you get lost, I will find you and pull you back to love. That's what writing does to me.

That simple promise holds a very significant purpose. If you have it with a person, a work, a community, or a home know that we are all in connection for a purpose, to lead each other to love itself. Distance doesn't matter. Birds of a feather flock together.

But you cannot walk the same path as they do. The work has its own journey and the individual in you has its own journey. We must know when we need to connect, when we need to go back home to ourselves. Rest, self care, and solitude are way more essential than we think they are.

They help you align. They give you enough strength to walk on your path, listen to your own voice, and reach your destination. Everything and everyone has their own map, their own itinerary, their own journey.

So do not let anything you love treat you like a priced possession. I can't command you, manipulate you, force you to be someone, make something out of you or control you. I am grateful for you, I respect you, I see you, You are fine just the way you are. I am just here to remind you of who you are. Bring the best of you closer to you and help you let go of everything you are not. Together or apart, we must remember to go home, to love itself. That's the little love I share with the work I am doing. I am sure it came my way to lead me home.

We all have to learn some very big lessons before we go there. We can do it slowly. One day at a time.

One path or infinite paths, we are all leading toward one love. We all appear different but, one way or another, merge into the same. If this book is in your hands, I believe your heart is already open. So, allow it to reveal itself. Rediscover and realign with yourself, your work, and your person.

Please do not get lost in what you love, but find your way through love to love itself.

I dare you!

So, one love.

Signing-off as Tejaswi Kolli
Beloved, bright, and blissfully aware.